Richard Price

The evidence for a future period of improvement in the

state of mankind

Richard Price

The evidence for a future period of improvement in the state of mankind

ISBN/EAN: 9783337132071

Printed in Europe, USA, Canada, Australia, Japan

Cover: Foto ©Suzi / pixelio.de

More available books at **www.hansebooks.com**

THE EVIDENCE

FOR A FUTURE

PERIOD OF IMPROVEMENT

IN THE STATE OF MANKIND,

WITH THE

MEANS AND DUTY OF PROMOTING IT,

REPRESENTED IN A

DISCOURSE,

DELIVERED ON

WEDNESDAY the 25th of APRIL, 1787,

AT THE

MEETING-HOUSE IN THE OLD JEWRY, LONDON,

TO THE SUPPORTERS OF A

NEW ACADEMICAL INSTITUTION

AMONG

PROTESTANT DISSENTERS.

By RICHARD PRICE, D.D. F.R.S.

LONDON:
PRINTED BY H. GOLDNEY,
FOR T. CADELL, IN THE STRAND; AND J. JOHNSON,
ST. PAUL'S CHURCH-YARD.

M DCC LXXXVII.

Juſt publiſhed by the ſame AUTHOR,

And printed for MR. CADELL.

SERMONS on the Chriſtian Doctrine as held by the different Denominations of Chriſtians;

TO WHICH ARE ADDED

SERMONS on the Security and Happineſs of a Virtuous Courſe, the Goodneſs of GOD, and the Reſurrection of Lazarus.

A

SERMON, &c.

MATTHEW vi. 10.

THY KINGDOM COME. THY WILL BE DONE ON EARTH AS IT IS IN HEAVEN.

THESE words, being a part of the Lord's prayer, muſt be perfectly familiar to you. It is evident that by the kingdom mentioned in them is meant, not that abſolute dominion of the Deity by which he does *whatever he pleaſes in the Armies of Heaven and among the inhabitants of the earth*; but that moral kingdom which conſiſts in the voluntary obedience of reaſonable beings to his laws, and, particularly, that kingdom of the Meſſiah which our Saviour came to eſtabliſh.

The same kingdom is undoubtedly here meant, with that which we are told in the Gospel History the apostles went about preaching every where and declaring to be at hand; which the Jews at the time this prayer was framed were impatiently expecting; and which in their religious services they were continually praying for in the words, *May his kingdom reign. May the Messiah come, and deliver his people.*

This kingdom is described, in the Prophecy of Daniel, under the character of a kingdom which the God of heaven was to set up in the time of the fourth temporal kingdom upon earth (or the Roman empire), and which was *to be given to the Son of Man, and* to increase gradually *till it broke in pieces all other kingdoms, and filled the whole earth.* In the prophecy of the seventy weeks the very time of the commencement of this kingdom is fixed; and it appears evidently that the phrases, *kingdom of God*, and *kingdom of heaven*, which the Jews used to signify the reign of their Messiah, and by which it is expressed in the New Testament, were derived from these prophetical representations in Daniel.

This

This petition, therefore, in our Lord's prayer, referred primarily to the introduction of the Christian religion among mankind. His disciples were directed by it, and by the petition that follows it (*thy will be done on earth as it is in heaven*), to pray, that the advent of his kingdom might be speedy, that the Gospel might be soon established in the world, that the virtue which it was fitted to inspire might take place every where, and mortal men be taught to regard God's will with a submission resembling that of the heavenly spirits. We cannot express before the Deity any desires that are more reasonable and important. The establishment of Christ's kingdom includes in it the enjoyment of the highest blessings that can be communicated to the world. It is a kingdom of light, and peace, and virtue. It is the beginning and foundation of an everlasting kingdom in the heavens. The subjects of it are fellow-citizens with angels, and heirs of a glorious immortality. With the utmost ardour then might the apostles and first disciples pray for the coming of this kingdom; and nothing can *now* be a juster object of the prayers of Christians.

For I cannot be of the opinion of those of our dissenting brethren who scruple using this prayer, from an apprehension that the words (*thy kingdom come*) cannot be used with propriety now the kingdom of Christ *is* come and the grace of the Gospel made known to men. The truth is, that there is a kingdom of Christ still to come. You should recollect that there are two comings of Christ's kingdom mentioned in the Scriptures, one *partial* and the other *universal*; and that though the former is past, yet we may with the utmost reason pray for the latter, and for that better state of things upon earth which our Lord expresses, by *doing the will of God on earth as it is done in heaven.*—Hitherto, the kingdom of the Messiah has been in its infancy. The most glorious period of it is yet future—His religion is now confined to a few nations. It will hereafter extend itself over all nations.—It is now dishonoured by much contention, superstition, and wickedness. Hereafter, it is to be cleared of these evils, and to triumph over all false religions.—Hitherto, it has caused the will of God to be done but very imperfectly. Hereafter, it will cause the

the will of God to be done on earth, as it is done in heaven.—The light it has hitherto produced has been like the dawn of the morning. It will hereafter produce a bright day over the whole earth.—In other words, and to ufe our Lord's comparifon in the parable of the grain of muftard feed; the kingdom of heaven has hitherto refembled a fmall feed germinating under ground. A period is coming in which it will throw off all that encumbers it, and grow up to a tree large enough for the birds of the air to lodge among its branches.

That fuch a ftate of chriftianity lies before us between this and the end of time; or, that there is a progreffive improvement in human affairs which will terminate in greater degrees of light and virtue and happinefs than have been yet known, appears to me highly probable; and my prefent bufinefs will be to reprefent to you the nature, the grounds, and the ufes of this expectation.—In doing this I fhall firft ftate the evidence which makes it probable; after which I fhall be naturally led to take notice of the means by which it is to be accomplifhed, and the encouragement it gives us in our

our exertions to promote the improvement of the world; and, particularly, in that undertaking which occasions the present service.

The evidence on which the expectation I have mentioned rests, is taken, partly, from tradition and scripture; and, partly, from reason and the necessary tendencies of things, confirmed by what we know of the *past* and see of the *present* state of the world.

There has been a tradition which has led Jews and Pagans (as well as Christians) to expect that the last ages of the world will be ages of improvement and happiness. This tradition is so ancient, and has been so general, that there is, I think, some regard due to it. But it is of little consequence compared with the declarations of scripture on this subject. These are clear and decisive. I have just mentioned a parable of our Lord's which directs our views to a future enlargement of his kingdom. To the same purpose is his comparison of his kingdom to a particle of leaven, which worked gradually and insensibly in a large quantity of meal, till the *whole* was leavened. St. Paul speaks in very plain language of a time when

when the *fullness of the Gentiles shall come in, and all Israel be saved.* Rom. ii. 25. Isaiah prophesies that, in the latter days, the mountain of the Lord's house shall be established on the top of the mountains, and all nations flock into it ; *and the Lord shall judge among the nations, and they shall beat their swords into plow-shares, and their spears into pruning-books. Nation shall not lift up a sword against nation, neither shall they learn war any more.* Isaiah ii. 2, 3, 4. The same prophet, in the eleventh and sixth chapters, foretells that under the reign of the Messiah, the *Lord would create new heavens and a new earth. The people of the Jews should be all righteous, and inhabit their land for ever. The wolf should dwell with the lamb, and the leopard lie down with the kid, and the lion eat straw with the ox, and the earth be filled with the knowledge of the Lord as the waters cover the sea.*—Daniel, in a passage already quoted, tells us, that the kingdom of the Messiah was *to break in pieces all other kingdoms,* and to encrease till it *filled the whole earth.*—In the seventh chapter he gives a particular account of a tyrannical power which was to appear after the fall of the Roman

man empire, and which, after continuing a limited time, was to be destroyed, and to be succeeded by an universal kingdom which should never be destroyed. This kingdom, according to Daniel's representation, is to be the *fifth* and last universal monarchy on earth; and he describes it under the character of the reign of the *saints*; that is, of an empire of reason and liberty and virtue which is to follow despotism, ignorance, and wickedness. *I beheld,* says he (verse 11.) *till the beast* (that is, the tyrannical power just mentioned) *was destroyed and given to the burning flame. And then came the Son of Man in the clouds of heaven; and there was given him dominion and glory, that all men and languages should serve him; and the kingdom, and dominion, and the greatness of the kingdom under the whole heaven, was delivered to the people of the saints of the Most High.* In the last chapter of this prophecy we have the remarkable declaration, that at the time of the end (till which time Daniel represents himself as ordered to seal his words) many should *run to and fro, and knowledge should be increased.*

St. Paul

St. Paul in his second Epistle to the Thessalonians assures us that the day of judgment would not come till an APOSTACY had taken place in the Christian church, and a *man of sin had appeared in it who should exalt himself above all that is called God, and whose coming should be after the working of Satan with signs and lying wonders, but whom the Lord would consume with the breath of his mouth and the brightness of his coming.* St. John tells us, that the *holy city* (by which undoubtedly is meant the Christian church) should be trodden under foot 1260 years; at the end of which term he represents the kingdoms of this world as becoming the kingdoms of the Lord and of his Christ. Rev. xi. 2, 15. *The beast and the false prophet*, he says, *will be taken and cast into a lake of fire* (that is, all antichristian corruption and oppression will be abolished), *and Christ shall reign a thousand years, and the saints shall reign with him.* That is; truth and righteousness shall for a long period become prevalent, and mankind universally receive and acknowledge Christ as their Head and Lawgiver.—I will only add our Lord's prediction in Luke xxi. 24. *The Jews shall be led captive*

tive to all nations, and Jerusalem shall be trodden down of the Gentiles till the times of the Gentiles are fulfilled. These words are very striking. They intimate to us a dispersion of the Jews for a certain period; the preservation of them through that period; and some great revolution in the state of the Gentiles at the end of it. It is evident that these predictions in the Old and New Testaments have the same events in view, nor is it possible with any appearance of reason to apply them to any events which have already happened. Certainly, the stone mentioned by Daniel which *was cut out of the mountain without hands* (that is, without the aid of human power) has not yet filled the whole earth. That man of sin who was to usurp the prerogatives of the Deity, and to deceive the world with lying miracles, has not yet been destroyed by the brightness of our Lord's second coming. The knowledge of the Lord has not yet covered the earth as the waters fill the channels of the sea. The universal empire of reason and virtue has not yet been established; nor have all people and nations been yet brought to serve the Son of Man. War has not yet been

been excluded from the world, nor has liberty taken place of tyranny, knowledge of ignorance, and sanctity of vice and corruption. To such a happy termination of human affairs in this world, next to the happiness of the heavenly state, the Scriptures point our views; and it is an argument in their favour, that they do give us an expectation so animating, amidst the variety of gloomy prospects with which this world, in its present state, is often presenting us; for it is an expectation no less credible and probable in itself than it is encouraging.— This is what I shall now proceed to shew you.

Almost every object in nature grows up gradually, from a weak and low, to a mature and improved state of being. The condition of mankind, in particular, has been hitherto improving. At first they were rude and ignorant. In time several of the arts were discovered. Civilization and agriculture began, and governments were established. By degrees the arts were improved. New ones were discovered, and better forms of government were established; and in the pre-

present *æra* of the world, it is evident, that the life of man appears with greater dignity than ever; and that in confequence of a vaſt variety of fucceſſive improvements and additions produced by them in the fources of human enjoyment, there is the fame difference between the ſtate of our ſpecies now and its ſtate at firſt, as there is between a youth approaching to manhood and a child juſt born.

It deferves particular confideration here, that it is the nature of improvement to increafe itfelf. Every advance in it lifts mankind higher, and makes them more capable of farther advances; nor are there, in this cafe, any limits beyond which knowledge and improvement cannot be carried. And for this reafon, difcoveries may, for aught we know, be made in future time, which, like the difcoveries of the mechanical arts and the mathematical fciences in paſt time, may exalt the powers of men and improve their ſtate to a degree, which will make future generations as much fuperior to the prefent as the prefent are to the paſt. Let us here look back again,

At

At the first establishment of civil society man was an animal, naked in body and mind; running about in the woods, or tending cattle, destitute of arts and laws and ideas. From this low condition he has risen to be the animal we now see him; to command the powers of nature; to fertilize the earth; to traverse the ocean; and to measure the distances and magnitudes of the sun and planets. His progress to this state has been irregular and various. Ages of improvement have been followed by ages of barbarism; and the several climates of the earth have felt the vicissitudes of knowledge and ignorance just as they have, of light and darkness. Yet what has been lost in one place, or at one time has been gained in another; and an age of darkness and barbarism has been succeeded by ages of improvement more rapid than any that preceded them. There was a time when no man was what whole countries are now. And there may come a time when *every* country will be what *many* are now; and when *some* will be advanced to a state much higher.

Nothing

Nothing can direct us better in judging of the manner in which future improvements are likely to proceed, than reflecting on the courfe of human improvement as it has hitherto taken place. I cannot illuftrate what I now mean better than by inftancing in natural philofophy.

The higheft ftate of philofophical and aftronomical knowledge was, at the beginning of this century, that which it had attained by the difcoveries of Sir Isaac Newton. But it had been the work of many ages to prepare mankind for thefe, and to bring the world to a capacity of underftanding and receiving them. To a few wife men above two thoufand years ago there appeared fome glimmerings of this philofophy, but they were difregarded and foon loft. A barbarous philofophy, called the *Peripatetic*, prevailed after this for a long period. The inventor of it (like the Pope in the Chriftian church) was fet up as an univerfal mafter, and the moft wretched jargon was received implicitly for true fcience. It is fcarcely poffible to defcribe the ftate of darknefs with refpect to the knowledge of nature, in which the world was involved

volved during this whole time. About two centuries ago a glimmering of light again appeared, and a more rational philofophy began to gain ground. The light gradually increafed. One great genius rofe after another, and one difcovery produced further difcoveries. A BACON was followed by a BOYLE, and a BOYLE by a NEWTON. Each of thefe prepared the way for his fucceffor; and the *laſt*, (the pride and glory of this country, and a name with which no names of kings and princes deferve to be thought of) the laſt, I fay, has ftruck out a glorious light. He extended on every fide the boundaries of fcience; fubjected light itfelf to diffection; and with a fagacity never before known among mortals, unfolded the laws which govern the folar fyftem. Such, however, were the prejudices in favour of former fyftems of philofophy, that even his philofophy, though founded on experiment and demonftration, was not immediately received. For many years it encountered much oppofition: But at laſt it made its way. Foreign nations came over to it; and it is now the philofophy of the world. A ſtate of philofophy fo improved could not

take

take place soon among mankind. It was necessarily reserved for an advanced age of the world. What is now known of the relation of this earth to the sun, and of the order of the heavenly bodies, is so contrary to vulgar prejudices, and seems to be so contradicted by the testimony of our senses, that had it been proposed, even to the philosophers of *Greece* and *Rome*, they would probably have scouted it as much as they did Christianity. False systems of philosophy have occasioned a more thorough examination of philosophical subjects; and their detection has given greater weight and stability to the true philosophy; for truth always shines brighter and stands firmer after growing out of the ruins of error; and an error once prevalent, and afterwards detected, is never likely to recover itself.

These observations are applicable with strict propriety to the natural course of improvement in *religious* knowledge; and, particularly, the knowledge of genuine Christianity and its spread among mankind. Till the time of our Saviour, the world had been too much in its infancy to be capable of admitting more of the knowledge of Christianity

Christianity than could be communicated by obscure hints, and a succession of dark preparatory dispensations. And even in the ages immediately following the time of our Saviour, it was by no means ripe for that universal prevalency of Christianity which we expect hereafter. The prejudices of mankind were then of such a nature, and the doctrines of the gospel so much out of the road of their ideas, that had it prevailed every where, it must have prevailed in a very imperfect form; and an adulteration of it by the false learning and philosophy of the times was unavoidable. For these reasons it might be necessary, that at first there should be only a partial propagation of it, and that its more general establishment should be deferred till the world was more improved, and therefore more capable of properly understanding it; till sufficient time had been allowed for a full discussion of its doctrines; till the completion of prophecy became an argument for it so striking, as to be irresistible; till the system of nature, and the plans of Providence should be laid more open to our views, and there should be a possibility of establishing it among

among mankind, in such purity, and with such evidence, as should leave no danger of farther adulterations of it.

It appears, therefore, that the same preparation of ages which is required to bring about advances in philosophical knowledge, is required also in religious knowledge. We are apt to be hasty and impatient. We should learn to wait till seeds have had time to grow and to produce crops. The government of the Deity proceeds gradually and slowly. As he does not bring the *individuals* of the human race on the stage of mature life, before they have been duly prepared for it, by passing through the instruction and discipline of infancy and childhood, so neither does he bring the species to that finished state of dignity and happiness for which it is intended, without a similar introduction and education.

Religious improvement must be expected to keep pace with other improvements. There is a connexion between all the different branches of knowledge which render this necessary. It would be strange, indeed, if men were not likely to understand religion best, when they understood best all

other

other subjects; or if an increase of *general* knowledge only left us more in the dark in theology. This is what those of our brethren who will admit of no new lights in religion would have us believe. But nothing can be more unreasonable. The age of polite literature in antient *Greece* and *Rome* was likewise the age when general knowledge prevailed most; and the period of the revival of letters in these last ages was also the period of the reformation from popery; and in like manner it must be expected, notwithstanding all the obstacles which the friends of old establishments endeavour to throw in the way, that the present period of more knowledge than ever yet existed in the world will produce a *farther* reformation.

It is observable that the Scriptures place the downfal of Antichrist before the commencement of the universal kingdom of the Messiah. This must be the order in which these events will happen. It would be absurd to imagine that Christianity, in its corrupt state, will ever become the universal religion. Previously to this it must lose that connection with civil power which has debased

based it, and which now in almost every Christian country turns it into a scheme of worldly emolument and policy, and supports error and superstition under the name of it. The absurdities fathered upon it must be exploded; and it must be displayed to the world in its native and original excellence. Then only will it be fit to triumph over false religions, and to reform and bless all nations.

The observations now made may be of use in assisting you to form just ideas of the progressive course of human improvement. Such has it hitherto been; and such the natures of things assure us it must continue to be. Like a river into which, as it flows, new currents are continually discharging themselves, it must increase till it becomes a wide-spreading stream, fertilizing and enriching all countries, and *covering the earth as the waters cover the sea.*

I will here point out to you briefly a few circumstances, in the present state of the world, which indicates a farther progress; and are particularly encouraging.

First.

First. In philosophical knowledge, great advances have been lately made. New fields of philosophy have been opened since the time of Sir Issac Newton. Our ideas of the extent and grandeur of the universe have been carried much farther than he carried them, and facts in the system of nature discovered, which could they have been intimated to him, would have been pronounced by him impossible. Standing on his shoulders and assisted by his discoveries we see farther than he did. How daring then would be the man who should say, that our successors will not see farther than we do?

This increase of natural knowledge must be accompanied with more enlarged views and liberal sentiments in religion; and we find that this has been its effect. There is, indeed, no circumstance in the present state of the world which promises more than the liberality in religion * which is now prevailing.

* This liberality is attended with one effect, which every good man must see with concern; I mean, an indifference to all religion, and a disposition to scepticism: but this may be an evil of short duration, and it will, probab-

vailing. God be thanked, the burning times are gone; and a conviction of the reasonableness of universal toleration is spreading fast. Juster notions also of the origin and end of civil government are making way; and an experiment is now making by our brethren on the other side of the Atlantic of the last consequence, and to which every friend of the human race must wish success. There a total separation of religion from civil policy has taken place, which will probably read a lesson to the world that will do it infinite service. Alliances probably, in the end prove advantageous rather than hurtful to the interest of true religion. It is less an evil than that wretched ignorance which has turned religion into a compromise with the Deity for ungoverned passions, and that frantic zeal for modes of faith which has led men to hate and destroy one another. Infidelity is occasioned by mistaking for Christianity that which is held out as such in the civil establishments of it. And this is an effect which will cease when the cause ceases. I will add, that the opposition to Christianity must (as I have observed above) be serviceable to it, by producing a stricter enquiry into its nature and evidence. I believe this, because I believe it to be of God. He who thinks otherwise must, if he is consistent, believe that it will not bear enquiry, and consequently, that it is *not* of God, and ought to be opposed.

ances between church and state and flavish hierarchies are losing credit, long experience having taught their mischief. The nature of religious liberty is better understood than ever. -In the last century, those who cried out the loudest for it meant only liberty for themselves because the advocates of truth. But there is now a conviction prevailing that all encroachments on the rights of conscience are pernicious and impious; that the proper office of the civil magistrate is to *maintain peace*; not to support *truth*.—To defend the *properties* of men, not to take care of their *souls*.—And to protect *equally* all honest citizens of all persuasions, not to set up one religious sect above another.

Sentiments so reasonable must continue to spread. They promise an open and free stage for discussion, and general harmony among the professors of Christianity. O happy time! when bigotry shall no more persecute the sincere enquirer, and every one shall tolerate as he would wish to be himself tolerated—When mankind shall love one another as brethren amidst their religious differences, and human authority in religion be exploded—When civil governors shall
know

know their duty and employ their power for its proper purpose—When the sacred blessing of liberty shall meet with no restraint except when used to injure itself; and all shall be allowed without the fear of losing any rights, to profess and practise that mode of faith and worship which they shall think most acceptable to their Maker. Then will come to pass the prophecy of Isaiah, (before recited to you) *The wolf will dwell with the lamb; the leopard lie down with the kid; and the lion eat straw with the ox. The sucking child shall play on the hole of the asp; and they shall not hurt or destroy in all the earth.*

I might now, would the time allow, proceed to recite many other important circumstances in the state of the world, which are preparations for that revolution in favour of human happiness, which is the object of this discourse. Such as the alleviation of the horrors of war occasioned by the spread of the principles of humanity; and the encouragement arising from hence, (and also from the growing conviction of the folly as well as the iniquity of wars) to expect a time when nation

nation shall no more lift up a sword against nation.—The softened spirit of popery; and the visible decline of the papal power.—The extinction of the order of Jesuits, and the demolition of convents and monasteries.—The shutting of the doors of the infernal inquisition, and the ceasing of acts of faith.—The extended intercourse between the different parts of the world; and the facility of the diffusion of knowledge created, first by the invention of the art of printing, but now carried farther than ever by the increase of commerce, and the improvements in the art of navigation.—The establishment, at this moment going forward, of an *equal* representation of the different provinces of FRANCE; and the tendencies to it in some of the other countries of EUROPE.—All these circumstances (and many more might be mentioned) render the present state of the world unspeakably different from what it was. They shew us man a milder animal than he was and the world outgrowing its evils, superstition giving way, antichrist falling, and the *Millennium* hastening.

Having stated to you the evidence for the doctrine which is the subject of this discourse,

course, I shall now proceed to what I next proposed when I entered upon it. I mean, to take notice of the means by which that happy termination of affairs on this globe which I have been representing is to be brought about. The observations I have made plainly point out to us these means; and, therefore, I have, in some measure, anticipated myself on this subject. There are, however, some of these means which I must not omit to recal to your remembrance, and to which it is necessary that, on the present occasion, I should more particularly direct your attention.

In general; it is obvious that this end is to be brought about by the operations of Providence concurring with those tendencies to improvement, which I have observed to be inseparable from the nature of man. Often Providence works for this end by bringing good out of evil, and making use of human passions to accomplish purposes contrary to those at which they aimed. It would be easy to mention many instances of this. The end of persecutors is to prevent the spread of heterodox opinions; but, instead of answering this end, it generally gives such opinions a wider spread. The progress

progress of Christianity has been assisted in this way; for it is a very just observation, that the blood of the martyrs has been the seed of the church. The political views of princes *have* often, and *are* now remarkably operating in the same way. The passions of King Henry the 8th, were the means of introducing that period of light and reformation in this country to which we owe our present liberty and happiness. The writings of unbelievers have done service to the Christian religion, by causing a stricter enquiry into its evidence, and clearing it of the rubbish which has been thrown upon it, and the false doctrines which have been mingled with it. And I am greatly mistaken, if the obstinacy with which abuses so gross as to be palpable to all the world are retained, in the present age, and even in this country, will not in the end prove a great public benefit by causing a more quick and complete overthrow of them, and of the establishments that support them, and thus giving a better opportunity for the introduction of establishments, favourable to truth and liberty and virtue.

Such are the secret and indirect means by which providence often carries on its ends. But,

But, in the present case, the most common means which it employs are the investigations and active exertions of enlightened and honest men. These are aimed directly at the melioration of the world, and without them it would soon degenerate. It is the blessing of God on the disquisitions of reason and the labours of virtue, united to the invisible directions of his Providence, that must bring on the period I have in view. Inactivity and sleep are fatal to improvement. It is only (as the prophet Daniel speaks) by *running to and fro*, that is, by diligent enquiry, by free discussion and the collision of different sentiments, that knowledge can be increased, truth struck out, and the dignity of our species promoted. Every one of us ought to co-operate with his neighbours in this great work, and to contribute all he can to instruct and reform his fellow-creatures. His power may be little; but this is no reason against exerting it as far as it will go. The less his power is, the more anxious he should be to employ that little, and not to suffer any part of it to be lost. There are none who have not some degree of power. The rich may help by

their

their fortunes. The great by their influence. The poor by their labour: And the learned by their inftruction and counfel. And were all to contribute all they can in thefe different ways much would be done; and the world would make fwift advances to a better ftate.

The obfervations I have made fhew that our exertions for this purpofe ought more efpecially to be directed to the following points.

Firft, An improvement in the ftate of civil government. The difpofitions and manners of men depend more than we can well conceive on the nature of the government to which they are fubject. There is nothing fo debafing as defpotic government. They convert the governed into *beafts*, and the men who govern into *demons*. Free governments, on the contrary, exalt the human character. They give a feeling of *dignity* and confequence to the governed, and to the governors a feeling of *refponfibility*, which has a tendency to keep them within the bounds of their duty, and to teach them, that they are more properly the *fervants* of the public than its *governors*.—Much ftudy has

has been employed, and much pains taken, to find out the beſt forms of government; nor is there any ſubject on which the human underſtanding can employ itſelf much more uſefully. Many improvements remain to be made; and it ſhould be the buſineſs of wiſe and good men to inveſtigate them, and to throw as much light as poſſible on a ſubject ſo intereſting to human happineſs *. I cannot help taking this opportunity to remove a very groundleſs ſuſpicion with reſpect to myſelf, by adding, that ſo far am I from preferring a government purely republican, that I look upon our own conſtitution of government, as better adapted than any other to this country, and, in

THEORY,

---

* Much aſſiſtance in this enquiry may be derived from the *Defence of the* AMERICAN *conſtitutions of government*, lately publiſhed by his Excellency Mr. ADAMS, where an account is given of moſt of the governments that have hitherto exiſted, in order to prove the neceſſity of providing checks and balances in a conſtitution of government, by lodging, as is done in our own conſtitution, the power of legiſlation in more than one aſſembly, and ſeparating from one another the legiſlative, executive, and judicial powers.

THEORY, excellent*. I have said in THEORY for, in consequence of the increase of corruption and the miserable inadequateness of our representation, it is chiefly the THEORY and FORM of our constitution that we possess; and this I reckon our first and worst and greatest grievance. We have been the most distinguished people under heaven. Lately our glory has been eclipsed. But could we, in this instance, turn the *form* into the *reality* (the *shadow* into the *substance*) we might recover our former rank; and, with the aid of *strong* measures for reducing our debts, rise, perhaps, to greater glory than ever.

But, I must hasten to what I meant next to mention as an object necessary to be attended to by the enlightened part of mankind,

---

* What I here say of myself I believe to be true of the whole body of *British* Subjects among Protestant Dissenters. I know not *one* individual among them who would not tremble at the thought of changing into a Democracy our mixed form of government, or who has any other wish with respect to it, than to restore it to purity and vigour, by removing the defects in our representation, and establishing that independence of the three states on one another, in which its essence consists.

kind, in order to improve the world. I mean, gaining an open field for difcuffion, by excluding from it the interpofition of civil power, except to keep the peace; by feparating religion from civil policy; and emancipating the human mind from the chains of church-authority, and church-eftablifhments. Till this can be effected, the worft impediments to improvement will remain *. The period to which I have been carrying

* Some notion of thefe impediments may be derived from the following facts. *Anaxagoras* was tried and condemned in *Greece* under a *Pagan* eftablifhment for teaching that the fun and ftars were not deities, but maffes of corruptible matter. Accufation of a like kind contributed to the death of Socrates. The threats of biggots, and the fear of becoming the fport of prefumptuous and ignorant men, prevented *Copernicus* from publifhing, for more than 30 years, the papers containing his difcovery of the true fyftem of the world; and after at laft giving permiffion to his friends to publifh them, he lived only to fee a copy of his book (in 1543) a few hours before his death. *Galileo* was obliged to renounce the doctrine of the motion of the earth, and fuffered a year's imprifonment for having afferted it. And fo lately as the year 1742, the beft commentary on the firft production of human genius (NEWTON's *Principia*) was not allowed to be printed at ROME, becaufe it afferted this doctrine; and the learned commentators were obliged

to

carrying your views muſt, as I have before obſerved to you, be preceded by the downfal of all ſlaviſh and antichriſtian hierarchies. Theſe *let at preſent, and they will let till they are taken away,* 2 Theſſ. ii. They are, by certain prophecy, deſtined to deſtruction. The liberality of the times has already looſened their foundations. The obſtinacy of their adherents is increaſing their danger; and the wiſe and virtuous of all deſcriptions ſhould make themſelves willing inſtruments in the hands of Providence to haſten their removal; not by any methods of violence; but by the diffuſion of knowledge, and the quiet influence of reaſon and conviction.

Thirdly; Another great object which the friends of reformation ought to attend to,

is

---

to prefix to their work (afterwards printed at GENEVA) a declaration, that on this point they ſubmitted to the deciſions of the church. The act of the firſt of Eliz. ch. 2. (which ſubſtituted our preſent eccleſiaſtical eſtabliſhment for the popiſh one which preceded it) was paſſed, Judge Blackſtone ſays, with the diſſent of all the Biſhops, (Gibſ. Codex 268.) and therefore the ſtyle of Lords Spiritual is omitted throughout the whole. Blackſtone's Comment. Book I. Chap. ii. Note.

is an IMPROVEMENT IN THE STATE OF EDUCATION.

The importance of Education has been so well represented to you by my excellent friend and brother, Dr. KIPPIS, in the discourse he delivered to you in this place last year, that it is needless for me to dwell much upon it. Nothing, certainly, can be of more importance. Seminaries of learning are the springs of society which, as they flow foul or pure, diffuse through successive generations depravity and misery, or on the contrary virtue and happiness. On the bent given to our minds as they open and expand, depends their subsequent fate; and on the general management of education depend the honour and dignity of our species. This is a subject with which we are far from being sufficiently acquainted. I often think there may remain a secret in it to be discovered which will contribute more than any thing to the amendment of mankind; and he who should advance one step towards making this discovery would deserve better of the world, than all the learned scholars and professors who have hitherto existed.

The

The courfe of improvement, when it has once begun, is (like the motion of a defcending body) an accelerated courfe. One improvement produces other improvements, and thefe others; and for this reafon there may be improvements, apparently little, which may lead to fo many more as to be, in their confequences, like the opening of new fenfes among mankind. There is great encouragement in this confideration. It fhews us, that the greateft good may arife from the flighteft degree of real improvement, which we can produce by our exertions; and it fhould, therefore, quicken our zeal in all fuch exertions.—This obfervation is, perhaps, more applicable to the fubject of education than any other. Improvement, in this cafe, muft be in the higheft degree ufeful. It has a particular tendency to perpetuate itfelf; and may, however inconfiderable at firft, increafe fo far as to bring about an univerfal reformation.—A fet of gentlemen, let us fuppofe, well-informed and of liberal fentiments, fee and lament the defects and abufes in the common modes of education. They refolve to try the effect of a new plan. They unite their

their influence and their contributions for this purpose. They found a college, small perhaps in its origin and narrow in its extent, but wise in its regulations. The care with which it is super-intended, and the excellence of its discipline, make it an *asylum*, in which young men are saved from the contagion to which they are exposed in other seminaries; and from which they go out well-instructed and well-principled, to be a comfort to their parents, an honour to their teachers, and blessings to Society. This soon engages general attention, and draws to it greater encouragement; in consequence of which it extends its beneficial influence through a wider circle. The example kindles zeal in others, and gives rise to institutions formed on plans still more extensive and improved. One generation thus improved communicates improvement to the next, and that to the next, till at last a progress in improvement may take place rapid and irresistible, which may issue in the happiest state of things that can exist on this earth.—It cannot be amiss for the gentlemen to whom I am addressing myself to fancy themselves in the situation now described.

scribed. Should it lead them to entertain a delusive expectation, it is a pleasing one, and they will have their reward. The success to which it carries their views is at least the tendency and the possible effect of their exertions. They have, hitherto, been encouraged beyond their expectations; and they have reason to look forward to greater encouragement. Let it appear, that they are likely to improve the state of education, and to sow the seeds of catholicism, virtue and rational piety in the kingdom; and there cannot be a doubt but they will receive all the support they can wish for. And who knows what a glorious service they may in the end perform? I feel, indeed, more and more of a hope that they are laying the foundation of an institution which will gather strength for a long period, and cause multitudes in future times to rise up and called them blessed.

One of the best effects which I expect from it, is an extension of that catholicism which I have just mentioned, and of a spirit of candour and benevolence. The common effect of education has hitherto been the reverse of this. It has taught a gloomy and
sour,

four, instead of a manly and benevolent religion; a religion consisting in a blind attachment to rites and forms and mysteries, and not in an impartial enquiry after truth, in the love of God and his creatures, and the practice of all that is worthy, from a regard to the moral government of the Deity and a future judgment. This has produced some of the worst consequences; and, particularly, that *Odium Theologicum* (that rancour of ecclesiastics) which, because surpassing in virulence all other rancour, has been long proverbial. There is, as I have before observed, less of this than there used to be in the world. But too much of it remains; nor will it be ever totally abolished, till a conviction becomes universal of the following truth. " That nothing is very " important except an honest mind; nothing " fundamental except righteous practise, " and a sincere desire to know and do the " will of God." I wish earnestly I could be, in any degree, the means of propagating this conviction. There is nothing by which any one can better serve the essential interests of society. The institution which occasions the present service will, I hope, do much

much good in this way. It is intended for the purpofe of providing that denomination of Proteftant Diffenters to which we belong, with a fucceffion of able and ufeful minifters. And this is of no lefs importance than the exiftence of our diffent from the eftablifhed church; a diffent which, in my opinion, is derived from the beft reafons,—from a diflike of the *creed* * as well as the

---

* It fhould be attended to, that I here fpeak of the *Prefbyterian* denomination of diffenters only. The whole body of Proteftant diffenters confifts of a great variety of different fects who have hardly *one common* principle of diffent. The majority of this very mixed and numerous body are, without doubt, *Calvinifts* and *Trinitarians*; and therefore cannot diflike the *creed* of the church; and, at the beginning of this century, the fame was true of even the *Prefbyterian* diffenters. A great revolution has taken place in the opinion of this laft clafs of diffenters: but it originated in the church itfelf with Sir ISAAC NEWTON, CLARKE, HOADLEY, WHISTON, SYKES, &c. and if from thefe diffenters the faith of the eftablifhed church is in any danger, it muft be more in danger from many of its own members.

I will take this opportuity to add, that there is a difference of opinion among diffenters on the fubject of civil eftablifhments of religion; fome approving them in general, and only difliking that particular form of religion which happens to be eftablifhed in this country; while

the *ceremonies* of the church—from a regard to Chrift as the only lawgiver in his kingdom, and the rejection of all human authority in religion—and, above all, from a conviction that the only proper object of our religious worfhip is, that one undivided and felf-exiftent Being and caufe of all caufes, who fent Chrift into the world, and who is *his* God and Father, no lefs than he is *our* God and father. Thefe are reafons which give the caufe we wifh to fupport, a dignity not to be expreffed; and render the prefervation of it our duty by all the means that are confiftent with the refpect we owe to our brethren of different fentiments; and particularly by the eftablifhment of an inftitution, like the prefent, for educating minifters.

But the education of minifters is far from being the only end of this inftitution. It is, (as the public has been informed in our printed reports) farther intended for

the

---

while others object to all fuch eftablifhments, and think, as I do, that they encroach on the rights of confcience, obftruct the progrefs of truth, engender ftrife and animofity, and turn religion into a trade. The former fort of diffenters muft wifh to fee their own religion fubftituted

the education of youth in general at that period of approach to mature life when they are moſt liable to ſeduction, and moſt in danger of taking a wrong turn.

In carrying on this undertaking, the firſt aim of its conductors will be undoubtedly to attach young minds as much as poſſible to virtue, and at the ſame time to communicate to them ſuch inſtruction as ſhall be beſt fitted to aſſiſt them in judging for themſelves, and to engage them to unite liberality and humility, to piety, zeal, and learning.

The beſt education is that which does this moſt effectually; which impreſſes the heart moſt with the love of virtue, and communicates the moſt expanded and ardent benevolence; which gives the deepeſt conſciouſneſs of the fallibility of the human underſtanding, and preſerves from that vile dogmatiſm ſo prevalent in the world; which makes men diffident and modeſt, attentive

ſtituted for that which is eſtabliſhed; but the latter dread ſuch a ſubſtitution, and can have no other wiſh than to ſee all unjuſt preferences on account of modes of faith and worſhip aboliſhed, and all honeſt and peaceable citizens equally protected and encouraged.

to evidence, capable of proportioning their assent to the degree of it, quick in discerning it, and determined to follow it; which, in short, instead of producing acute casuists, conceited pedants, or furious polemics, produces fair enquirers endowed with that heavenly wisdom described by St. James, *which is first pure, then peaceable, gentle, easy to be entreated, full of mercy and good fruits, without partiality and without hypocrisy.* An education so conducted is the only means of gaining free scope for the progress of truth; of exterminating the pitiful prejudices we indulge against one another; and of establishing *peace on earth and goodwill amongst men.*

Think here of the effects of education as commonly managed. Its business is to teach a learning which puffs up, and which must be unlearnt before reason can acquire its just influence. Instead of opening, it contracts. Instead of enlightening it darkens; and, by giving a notion of sacredness in disputable doctrines and stuffing the mind with prejudices, incapacitates for the reception of real wisdom, and makes men think it their duty to silence, to imprison, and perhaps to kill

kill one another in order to do God service. Such was the effect of education in our Saviour's time among Jews and Pagans. It made self-righteous Pharisees, ostentatious disputants, proud sophists, and cruel persecutors, zealous for the absurdities of superstition and idolatry, and furnished with skill to defend them and to resist conviction. And the consequence was that, not suspecting the necessity of knowing themselves fools before they could be wise, they rejected with disdain the instruction of the Gospel, and that the poorest and plainest men who had never been taught in their schools, or been perverted by the false learning of the times, entered into the kingdom of God before them. It is on this circumstance that our Lord's thanksgiving in *Matth.* xi. 25. is grounded. *I thank thee, O father, Lord of heaven and earth, because thou hast hid these things from the wise and prudent, and revealed them unto babes.* Let the conductors of this institution take care to avoid this error. Let it be their study to form men who shall, in Christ's sense, be *babes* rather than *wise and prudent*; that is, who shall possess the modesty, lowliness, and teachable simplicity of

G 2 children,

children, rather than the pride and dogmaticalnefs of men who, having been educated in colleges, think themfelves wife and learned; but whofe learning produces a worfe entanglement of the underftanding than common men are fubject to, and is nothing but deeper ignorance and more inveterate prejudice. This is the great advantage by which I wifh this inftitution to be diftinguifhed; and it is an advantage which it muft poffefs, if your prefent views are carried into execution. It is to be formed on an open and liberal plan. Our two univerfities are fortreffes erected for the fecurity and prefervation of the church of England, and defended for that purpofe by tefts and fubfcriptions. Moft of the feminaries alfo among ourfelves are intended for conveying inftruction in the particular fyftems of the fects that fupport them, and for making baptifts, independents, Calvinifts, and *orthodox* believers. The founders of *this* inftitution, while they neglect no proper means of making good fcholars and enlightened philofophers, will, I doubt not, be anxious above all things about making

good

good men, upright citizens, and *honest* and *candid* believers.

This is a defign that all muft approve who do not think, that the truth having been happily found out and eftablifhed in this kingdom two hundred years ago, nothing remains to be done but to fupport it, and to adopt meafures for maintaining the belief of it, and for creating an inviolable attachment to it. Thus, did Jews and Pagans think in our Saviour's time; and, therefore, rejected the Divine light of Chriftianity. Thus do *Mahometans* and *Papifts* now think of their national eftablifhments; and, therefore, continue in darknefs and fuperftition. Is it credible that like confequences fhould not arife from like fentiments in this country? Is it not as proper in *us*, as it would be in *them*, to *fufpect* our public creeds and forms? Can it be imagined, that we have reached a degree of perfection which renders farther enquiry needlefs? I am indeed much miftaken if fome very great errors do not ftill make a part of our national faith. This is, at leaft, poffible; and this *poffibility* is a fufficient reafon for maintaining an opennefs to conviction with refpect to it. Should fuch

errors

errors exist, and the reformed churches themselves want reformation, institutions for liberalizing education must do infinite good by being the means of detecting them. But should they not exist, still the best consequences must follow. It will appear that our national code of faith and worship can stand the test of examination. It will gain credit, and find a more honourable support than that authority of fallible men and that interference of secular power in religion, which have hitherto, almost every where, supported nothing but imposture, superstition and idolatry.

It may be objected, that the liberality in education which I have recommended, will have a tendency to set men loose from *all* principles. The observation I have just made proves this to be an unreasonable apprehension. The best way, certainly, of attaching men to *true* principles is to enable them to examine impartially *all* principles. Every truth that is necessary to be believed and really *sacred*, must be attended with the clearest evidence. Free enquiry can be hostile to nothing but absurdity and bigotry. It is only falshood and delusion which fly
from

from difcuffion, and chufe to fkulk in the dark.

But I am in danger of wandering beyond the proper purpofe of this difcourfe. Let me now recall briefly to your attention fome of the reafons which fhould quicken your zeal in the great work you have undertaken.

I have already taken notice of its great importance. Forming youthful and tender minds to virtue, and pointing their ambition to that moral excellence and refemblance of the Deity, which alone conftitute true honour and dignity—directing their faculties as they open, and checking in them the rifings of criminal paffions—affifting them in the acquifition of valuable knowledge, and teaching them habits of patience, modefty, candour, and felf-government—guarding them againft the influence of the foolifh prejudices which blind mankind, and preparing them by judicious difcipline and inftruction for an eafy admiffion of the light of truth; and thus contributing to the progreffive improvement of the world, the enlargement of Christ's kingdom, and the arrival of a period when the will of God will be done on earth, as it is in heaven.——This, brethren, THIS is a work of the noblest and highest nature. Angels can hardly be more usefully or honourably employed.

But consider next, the need there is of your exertions in this instance. It is a narrow and ill-managed education that keeps up discord and malevolence, and that produces most of the evils of life. It is this that is continually sending out into the world coxcombs, pedants, bigots, despots, and libertines, to debase the dignity of man, to embroil society, and to perpetuate ignorance, vice and slavery. The smallest degree of success in an attempt to correct these evils, by an improvement in the state of education, would be an ample reward for the greatest trouble and expence that could attend it. The inattention to this subject which has prevailed, is no less astonishing than melancholy. When the resolution * was taken to establish this institution,

* Soon after this resolution was taken, a body of very respectable Dissenters at Manchester, instead of joining us,

tion, there was but one seminary for education, after passing through the common grammar schools, to which we, as Dissenters of the denomination commonly, (though improperly) called *Presbyterian*, could look; and even this seminary was by the founder of it intended to form *Independents* and *Calvinists*. The moderation and wisdom of its *trustees* and *tutors* have indeed given it a liberal turn, and made it very useful. It is not, however, of sufficient extent to answer all our views. Being situated in the country, it wants many advantages which can be found only near the centre of the kingdom.——But I will not enter on a repetition of what you have so well observed on this subject in your reports and circular letters.

Let me, therefore, desire you, in the next place, to consider the obligation under which your constant use of the words of my

us, resolved on an attempt to establish a similar institution in that town. At first it was feared, that, by dividing our strength, this would weaken it too much; but the contrary seems now to appear, and there is reason to hope that both institutions will prosper.

my text lays you, and the encouragement it gives you.—To pray for a benefit, without using our endeavours to procure it, is a mockery of the Deity and an abuse of prayer. We are commanded to pray for our daily bread; but he that should do this, while he takes no pains to get his daily bread, would be inexcuseable. We are, therefore, bound by our use of that part of the Lord's Prayer which I have taken for my text, to employ all the means in our power to cause the kingdom of God to come, and his will to be done on earth as it is done in heaven. And one of the best of all the means we can employ is, I have shewn, the establishment of such a seminary as we have now in view.

Our use of this part of the Lord's Prayer is farther an *encouragement* to us in employing these means. A command to pray for a blessing, implies that we shall obtain it, if we use the means. In the present instance particularly, it assures us, that an extension of Christ's kingdom and an amendment of the state of the world, are blessings which lie in some degree within our reach,

and

and that our exertions for this purpose shall be favoured and succeeded.

The encouragement derived from hence is greatly increased by the doctrine on which I have been insisting. A more prosperous state of things is to take place on this earth. The stone which was cut out of the mountain, without human force, is hereafter to fill the whole earth, and the kingdom of the Messiah to become universal. Reason and Scripture lead to this expectation ‡. Remember then in your endeavours to enlighten

---

‡ "Let us," says the Marquis of CONDORCET excellently, "be cautious not to despair of the human "race. Let us dare to foresee, in the ages that will "succeed us, a knowledge and a happiness of which "we can only form a vague and undetermined idea.— "Let us count on the *perfectibility* with which nature "has endowed us; on the strength of the human "genius, from which long experience gives us a right "to expect prodigies; and let us console ourselves for "not being the living witnesses of that happy period, "by the pleasure of predicting and anticipating it, and "perhaps by the more sweet satisfaction of having by a "few moments accelerated its arrival." See page 365 of the Translation of the Marquis of CONDORCET's Account of the Life of M. TURGOT, late Comptroller-General of the Finances of FRANCE, printed for Mr. Johnson in St. Paul's Church-yard.

en and reform mankind, that you are cooperating with providence; that the hand of God has marked out your path; and that his favour will guide and protect you. I have been shewing you how much the state of the world encourages you. A spirit of enquiry is gone forth. A disdain of the restraints imposed by tyrants on human reason prevails. A tide is set in. A favourable gale has sprung up. Let us seize the auspicious moment, obey the call of Providence, and join our helping hands to those of the friends of science and virtue.— Think not, however, that you have no difficulties to encounter. It will not be strange if an alarm should be taken about the danger of the church. There is a jealousy natural to church establishments (especially when undermined by time and the spread of knowledge) which may produce such an alarm. In this case it would be a most unreasonable alarm, for if our religious establishment can bear discussion, and stands on good ground as its friends must believe, what harm can be done to it by an institution, the design of which is, not to inculcate the peculiarities of any sect, but to communicate

municate such general instruction, and to promote such a spirit of enquiry and candour, as shall form worthy citizens for the state, and useful ministers for the church?—This, however, is a consideration that will not prevent opposition. The enemies of reformation may be alarmed. Ignorance and intolerance may clamour. But their opposition cannot be successful. The liberal temper of the times must overpower them. Bigotry and superstition must vanish before increasing light. We see the clouds scattering. We live in happier times than our fore-fathers. The shades of night are departing. The day dawns; and the Sun of righteousness will soon rise with healing in his wings. Let us keep our attention fixed on this reviving prospect. Animated by it, let us persevere in our exertions, knowing that, as far as we are on the side of liberty and virtue, we are on that side which must at last prevail.

Let us, however, at the same time take care not to forget a caution which I have before given, and cannot too often repeat. While we proceed in our exertions with perseverance and zeal, let them be accompanied

panied with peaceablenefs, and difpofitions perfectly charitable.—Some of our fellow-chriftians are eagerly maintaining a pre-eminence in the Chriftian church, which Chrift has prohibited; and ftruggling to preferve the power they claim as interpreters of Chrift's laws, and kings in his kingdom*. They either do not fee the great change that is going forward; or, if they *do* fee it, they have not the wifdom to fuit their conduct to it, and to prepare for its effects.—Others of our brethren continue to hold as facred fome of the doctrines of the dark ages. The mift, which opening day is difperfing, ftill lurks round them. Imagining

* Never was a more important fervice done to the caufe of religious liberty, than by the excellent Bifhop *Hoadley*, in the controverfy occafioned by a fermon in which he confuted thefe claims. For this fermon, (and alfo his oppofition to a teft law which ftigmatizes a large body of the king's beft fubjects, and profanes a chriftian ordinance) he was threatened with the vengeance of both houfes of convocation; but the power of government (in this cafe wifely applied to the reftraint of clerical refentment) interpofed and faved him. The iffue is well known. *He* was promoted, and the CONVOCATION ruined; for fince that time it has never been allowed to fit to exercife its former powers.

gining the acceptance of the Deity to be confined within the circle of their own faith, they cannot view mankind with the same satisfaction that we do. They have not yet felt the chearing power of a religion which makes nothing effential but an honeft heart; and they look, perhaps, with pain on your attempts to ferve the caufe of truth and piety. But though, in this refpect lefs happy than ourfelves and as we think not fo well informed, they may be truly worthy; and we fhould learn not to condemn them, whatever fentiments, with refpect to us, a miftaken Judgment may lead them to entertain.

My own experience has induced me to fpeak thus to you. I have been an object of cenfure for actions which I confider as fome of the beft in my life. But being confcious that I have meant well, and believing that I have not laboured quite in vain, the cenfure I have met with has made no impreffion upon me. I look back with complacency; and I look forward with joy, in hope of a time when thofe good men who now diflike me on account of the difference of our religious opinions

and

and views, will be as ready to embrace me as I am to embrace them.

Excuse this digression. I am growing too tedious, and I have gone beyond my strength. I will therefore, conclude with directing you to carry your thoughts to another world. The period on which I have been discoursing will pass while we are silent in the grave. But through the grace of God in the great Redeemer, we shall be raised up from death and enter on a new world. THERE a brighter scene than this world can exhibit to us in its best state, will open upon us. THERE a government of consummate order will be established; and all the faithful and worthy of all religions will be gathered into it. THERE peace and love will reign in full perfection; and those who, by such exertions as yours, are the means of enlarging the kingdom of Christ, and causing the will of God to be done on earth as it is done in heaven, will be exalted to a happiness greater than can be now conceived, and which will never come to an end.—To this happiness, may God of his infinite mercy bring us, through Jesus Christ our Lord and Saviour.

F I N I S.

NOTE omitted at the words, *Connexion with civil power*, in page 19.

* It is necessary, in order to prevent mistakes, I should here observe, that by the *civil establishment of religion* which, in this and some other parts of this discourse, I have had in view, I mean an exclusive support, attended with exclusive advantages and emoluments, granted by civil power to the professors of *one particular* mode of faith and worship at the expence of all the members of the state, whether they *do* or *do not* approve that mode of faith and worship; and that, consequently, an *equal* support of religion in general, by requiring a contribution for that purpose, payable by every citizen, but with liberty to apply it to the support of that worship he likes best, as now practised in NEW ENGLAND; is not such an establishment of religion as I have intended to condemn. I must add, however, that, in my opinion, this is the farthest a legislature ought to go in its interference with religion. And, as all that is most important in religion is common to all religions (that is, the belief of a moral governor of the world and a future retribution) this seems to be the only method a legislature can take to encourage what is *salutary* in religion without injustice and oppression. If civil governors go farther, universal experience proves that, not being judges of religious truth, they will support falshood, obstruct the improvement of the world, and hurt the best interests of society.

REPORT, &c.

LONDON, *July* 21, 1786.

AT a numerous and respectable Meeting of the Subscribers to a New ACADEMICAL INSTITUTION among PROTESTANT DISSENTERS, for the education of their Ministers and Youth, THOMAS ROGERS, Esq. was called to the Chair; and the Resolutions of the last General Meeting of March 10th having been read and unanimously confirmed, the following Report from the Committee was read: viz.

GENTLEMEN,

YOUR Committee have taken the liberty of now convening you, in order to inform you of the progress they have made in the important business with which you entrusted them. They cannot reflect on the liberality and zeal, with which the NEW ACADEMICAL INSTITUTION has been encouraged, without peculiar satisfaction: And they have full confidence, that the Report, which they are now able to make, of the success of their application in its favour, will give you equal pleasure. Your Committee consider this success as a public testimony to the importance of that plan of education, which you concur in promoting; and as a happy omen of its establishment on a durable foundation, and of the extensive benefits that are likely to result from it.

As nothing deserves the attention of the Public in general, and of Protestant Dissenters in particular, more than the principles and character of their Youth; it seems

seems strange that no such Institution as that now proposed, uniting education with domestic government, and extending the advantages of both, to lay-students as well as to candidates for the Ministry, should have been hitherto established in the neighbourhood of London; and that the liberality and public spirit of the Dissenters, so distinguished on a variety of other occasions, should never have been directed to this great object. The want of such a provision for the education of our laity in particular has often been the subject of complaint; and it is, indeed, an evil which there has been great reason to lament. A spirit of free inquiry is now generally diffused; and wherever it prevails, it revolts against those restrictions and shackles, which embarrass the integrity and obstruct the improvement of youthful minds. In the present advanced state of science and of religious liberty, there are many unconnected with us as Dissenters, who, we are persuaded, will rejoice in the establishment and success of that liberal system of education and of domestic discipline, which is the object of our Institution: And some of them have already afforded us considerable support. You will permit us to add, Gentlemen, that there is ample encouragement to proceed, with steady and active exertion, in accomplishing, to its utmost extent, the design which you are countenancing by your presence and by your contributions.

In pursuance of the instructions of a General Meeting, held in this place on the 10th of March, your Committee opened a subscription in London, and circulated proposals for it through different parts of the kingdom: And they have now the pleasure to report to you, that the amount of the donations, the principal part of which has been already received and invested in the funds, is SEVEN THOUSAND pounds, fifteen shillings; and that of the Annual Subscriptions SIX HUNDRED and SIXTY-FIVE pounds, fourteen shillings and sixpence.

You will observe, Gentlemen, in examining the list now delivered to you, that it contains the names of many respectable persons in various parts of the country, who concur in testifying their approbation of our
Design,

Defign, and in liberally promoting the execution of it. We are not unapprized, that, notwithftanding our utmoft affiduity, there are many more, both in Town and Country, to whom we have not been able to communicate our propofals; and who will, without doubt, come forward, and unite their exertions to ours in the accomplifhment of a plan that is intended for general utility. We can hardly fuppofe, that any, who are not influenced either by miftaken views or an improper fpirit, can be active in their oppofition to it. No confiderate and candid perfon, we prefume, can openly avow himfelf hoftile to a Defign, that has no other object but the benefit of our youth, of our churches, and of the community in general.

We are affured, Gentlemen, from the difpofition to ferve the Inftitution which you have already difcovered, that you will avail yourfelves of every opportunity that may occur for increafing the number of its Friends. It is needlefs to ftate to you, that though the affiftance which has been received is liberal and encouraging, it requires a large increafe, in order to render it fully adequate to the great expence, that muft unavoidably attend the firft eftablifhment of an Inftitution which fhall be worthy of the generofity of its friends, refpectable in its connection with that body of Diffenters who are engaged in founding and fupporting it, extenfive in its benefits, and permanent in its duration. We hope, therefore, that thofe with whom you are to entruft the future conduct and final accomplifhment of the plan which has been adopted, will endeavour to procure farther aids for its fupport, by recommending it to fuch of the liberal-minded among their acquaintance as may not yet be fufficiently informed concerning it.

Your Committee have not been inattentive to a variety of other circumftances, that are effentially connected with the eftablifhment and future profperity of the Inftitution. They have been indefatigable in their endeavours to procure a houfe, in a fituation agreeable to the views of the Benefactors and Subfcribers, and fit for accommodating a fufficient number of Students. But notwithftanding the moft diligent fearch and inquiry, they have not hitherto been able to find any houfe house that is at all adapted to the purpose. It is, therefore, their opinion, that it will be thought necessary to build a commodious Academical House : And that this is the most practicable, and, all circumstances considered, the most eligible, and, probably, the most frugal measure. They also apprehend, that the parts adjacent to Hackney or Clapton would, for a variety of reasons which it is unnecessary to enumerate, be convenient in respect of situation : And they have reason to believe, that a proper spot of ground may be obtained in that neighbourhood. In the mean while your Committee are of opinion, that suitable apartments should be procured for one year, for the purpose of giving lectures to such divinity-students as the General Committee may think proper to encourage, until the Institution be fixed in a house capable of admitting a resident Tutor and the Students in general, at the beginning of the session 1787.

Your Committee farther inform you, that they have applied by a particular letter to each of the Trustees and Subscribers of the late Warrington Academy, and also by a memorial addressed to them at their General Meeting on the 29th of June : And they have the satisfaction to add, that the Trustees and Subscribers have been so obliging as to assign to the New Academical Institution their Philosophical Apparatus, and a moiety of the surplus of their remaining funds, under certain restrictions.

Application has likewise been made to the Trustees of the late Academy at Exeter for the use of their library, which your Committee have reason to believe will be attended with success.

The 23d Resolution of the 10th of March, which expresses that " a permanent fund is of great importance " to the prosperity and continued subsistence of this " institution," appeared to your Committee of such moment as to deserve their particular attention. You, Gentlemen, we are persuaded, will excuse our anticipating a business, which is referred by that Resolution to the General Committee ; and allow us to submit to your approbation some regulations with respect to such a fund, which we are of opinion it may be proper to adopt.

adopt. We are happy to think, that the liberality of the friends of the Inſtitution empowers us to make an immediate appropriation of part of our capital to this fund ; and that we ſhall be able to reſerve ſuch a proportion of future benefactions for this purpoſe, as to render this not only a permanent, but an increaſing fund.

Your Committee now beg leave to recommend the choice of a General Committee, agreeably to your Reſolutions of the 10th of March, who, we doubt not, will devote much of their time and attention to the completion of the great object which we have in view. Wiſdom, unanimity, and zeal, are neceſſary to perfect your Deſign: And we truſt that every exertion will be made, by thoſe to whom you commit the eſtabliſhment of your Inſtitution, for enſuring its credit and proſperity ; and that, conſcious of the integrity of their views, and encouraged by the magnitude and importance of the object, as well as by the concurrence of thoſe whoſe approbation is of the greateſt value, they will perſevere in ſo good a cauſe. The hope of its anſwering the important and uſeful ends, which you propoſe, and of its conducing to the extenſive and laſting benefit of Proteſtant Diſſenters and of the community in general, muſt animate every friend of religion and liberty, of his country and of mankind.

The Report of the Committee having been read, the Chairman made the following Report, viz.

Gentlemen,

I beg leave to inform you, that in purſuance of the 14th Reſolution of the 10th of March, application has been made to the Gentlemen therein named, requeſting their aſſiſtance for carrying on the purpoſes of the Inſtitution, as Tutors. I have now the pleaſure to acquaint you, that Dr. Price will aſſiſt in giving lectures on ſelect parts of Morals, Mathematics, Aſtronomy, and Natural Philoſophy : Dr. Kippis has conſented to lecture on the Belles Lettres, including Univerſal Grammar, Rhetoric, Chronology, and Hiſtory: Dr. Rees has undertaken Divinity, Hebrew, Jewiſh Antiquities,

quities, Ecclefiaſtical Hiſtory, and lectures on other ſubjects preparatory to the Miniſtry: And Mr. Worthington has undertaken Logic and Claſſical Literature. Dr. Rees and Mr. Worthington have alſo engaged to inſtruct the Students in the elementary parts of Mathematics and Natural Philoſophy in the enſuing year, until the arrangement of Tutors for the New Inſtitution can be completed, and the whole plan carried into full execution by the erection of a proper building.

I am directed farther to inform you, Gentlemen, that the Committee recommend particular attention to the inſtruction of the Students in Experimental Philoſophy, Chemiſtry, and a proper mode of elocution.

After theſe reports the following Reſolutions were propoſed and unanimouſly agreed to, viz.

I. Whereas by the 2d Reſolution of the 10th of March it was reſolved, that ſome farther regulations be adopted as to thoſe who ſhall become Annual Subſcribers after the 24th of June, it is now reſolved, in order to accommodate ſuch perſons as have not yet had an opportunity of ſubſcribing to the New Academical Inſtitution, that the payment of two, three, four, or five guineas, or upwards, before the 25th of December next, as an Annual Subſcription, ſhall conſtitute an Annual Governor: But that, after the 25th of December, the firſt payment of five guineas or upwards, the ſecond payment of four guineas, the third payment of three guineas, and the fourth payment of two guineas, each as an Annual Subſcription, ſhall be neceſſary to conſtitute Annual Governors.

II. That one-third of the preſent and future donations, benefactions, and bequeſts to the New Academical Inſtitution in the neighbourhood of London, the ſame not being Annual Subſcriptions, ſhall go to create a permanent fund; the capital whereof ſhall be preſerved for ever inviolable and unalienable in the hands of Truſtees.

III. That on the 1ſt of January in each year, the Treaſurer ſhall make up an account of all ſuch donations, benefactions, and bequeſts, not being Annual

Annual Subscriptions, as shall have been received in the preceding year, and deliver the same to the General Committee at their next ensuing Meeting; that one-third of the amount thereof may be passed or placed by the General Committee to the account of such fund.

IV. THAT the Annual income arising from the permanent fund shall alone be paid from time to time, as it arises, towards the support of the said Institution, in such manner as the General Committee shall direct; or, if the said Institution shall at any time hereafter be dissolved, or be discontinued for the space of three years, to the founding or to the support of any other Academical Institution, or of any Institution preparatory to such among the Protestant Dissenters, for the liberal education of youth in any part of England or Wales; or in giving exhibitions to Students for the Ministry; or in supporting one or more Tutors at any such Institution or Institutions within the same limits; as the General Committee shall direct.

V. THAT in case of the dissolution or suspension for three years of the said Institution, and after the discharge of its debts, all other property belonging to the said Institution, which shall then be subject to the disposal of the General Committee, shall be held in trust by the Trustees to be chosen in pursuance of the 7th Resolution of the General Meeting of the 10th of March last, jointly with the Trustees of the permanent fund; and that such other property shall thenceforth be applied to the same objects and by the same authority as the income of the permanent fund.

VI. THAT the General Committee establish the permanent fund, as soon as possible, agreeably to the preceding Resolutions; and that they prepare a proper declaration or deed of Trust for this purpose. That four Gentlemen, who are Governors for life, be appointed Trustees of the said fund, and that they be authorized to invest the monies belonging to it in land, stocks, buildings, or mortgages, and to vary and transpose the securities,

ties, under the direction of the General Committee, as circumstances may require. That all vacancies in this Trust shall be filled up by the General Meeting. And that the following Gentlemen be the first Trustees, viz. Mr. Joseph Travers, Mr. John Towgood, Mr. William Esdaile, and Mr. Thomas Rogers, jun.

VII. THAT in pursuance of the 4th Resolution of the 10th of March, the following Gentlemen be the General Committee, viz.

Levy Ames, Esq.
Nath. Barnardiston, Esq.
Dr. Bayly
Henry Beaufoy, Esq. M. P.
Benjamin Boddington, Esq.
Richard Bright, Esq.
George Brooksbank, Esq.
R. Hall Clarke, Esq.
Richard Cooke, Esq.
Michael Dodson, Esq.
Sir James Esdaile, Alderman
John Finch, Esq.
Edward Grubb, Esq.
William Hawker, Esq.
Christ. Heinekin, Esq.
Sir H. Hoghton, Bart. M.P.
T. Brand Hollis, Esq.
B. B. Hopkins, Esq. M. P.
Rev. T. Jervis,
George Jeffery, Esq.
Edward Jeffries, Esq.
Adam Jellicoe, Esq.
John Ingram, Esq.
Francis Kemble, Esq.
Andrew Kippis, D. D.
Thomas Lees, Esq.
Rev. T. Lindsey,
Rev. J. Lindsay,
Philip Mallet, Esq.
George Maltby, Esq.

Rev. T. Morgan,
W. Newman, Esq. & Ald.
Robert Newton, Esq.
Richard Price, D. D.
Abraham Rees, D. D.
Thomas Rickards, Esq.
Thomas Rogers, Esq.
William Ruffel, Esq.
John Savery, Esq.
William Scullard, Esq.
Samuel Shore, Esq.
Samuel Shore, jun. Esq.
Rev. J. Simpson,
Philip Slater, Esq.
William Smith, Esq. M. P.
Isaac Solly, Esq.
Thomas Streatfield, Esq.
William Tayleur, Esq.
R. G. Temple, Esq.
Matthew Towgood, Esq.
Joseph Turton, Esq.
Mr John Wansey,
George Webster, Esq.
James West, Esq.
Isaac Wilkinson, Esq.
Rev. Ed. Williams, Notting.
T. Carill Worsley, Esq.
Rev. H. Worthington, jun.
John Yerbury, Esq.

VIII. THAT

VIII. THAT the following Gentlemen be Correspondent Members of this Society: viz. the Rev. Messrs.

R. Alderson, Norwich
Edward Armstrong, Bath
R. Barbauld, Warwick-court
Malachi Blake, Taunton
Samuel Blythe, Birmingham
John Coates, ditto
J. Disney, D.D. Brumpton
Peter Emans, Coventry
W. Enfield, LL.D. Norwich
— Estlin, Bristol
Hugh Farmer, Walthamstow
J. Fuller, Chesham, Bucks
S. Griffiths, Wolverhampton
R. Harris, Colchester
W. Hawkes, Birmingham
P. Jillard, near Taunton
W. Johnstone, Brighthelmst.
George Morgan, Yarmouth
James Pickbourn, Hackney
— Pope, Stand, near Manch.
J. Priestley, LL.D. Birmingh.
R. Scolefield, ditto
— Walker, Enfield
G. Walker, Nottingham
W. Walters, Wimbledon
William Wood, Leeds
H. Worthington, Leicester
T. Wren, D.D. Portsmouth
John Yates, Liverpool.

IX. THAT in pursuance of the 7th Resolution of the 10th of March, the following four Gentlemen be Trustees, viz. Nathaniel Barnardiston, Esq. William Smith, Esq. M.P. Samuel Shore, jun. Esq. and Mr. John Wansey.

X. THAT in pursuance of the 8th Resolution the following three Gentlemen be the Committee of Treasury, viz: Thomas Rogers, Esq. Matthew Towgood, Esq. and Michael Dodson, Esq.

XI. THAT in pursuance of the 9th Resolution the following three Gentlemen, being Governors, but not of the General Committee, be Auditors of the Accounts of this Society, viz. Mr. Isaac Thompson, Mr. William Stone, and Mr. Sturch.

XII. THAT the Thanks of this Meeting be given to the Trustees and Subscribers of the late Warrington Academy for granting their Philosophical Apparatus and a moiety of the surplus of their remaining funds to the New Academical Institution: And that the Chairman be desired to transmit the same to Thomas Butterworth Bayley, Esq. the Chairman of the late Meeting, held at Warrington on the 29th of June.

B   XIII. THAT

XIII. THAT the thanks of this Meeting be given to the late Committee for their services.

XIV. THAT the thanks of this Meeting be given to the Chairman.

(Signed)

THOMAS ROGERS, Chairman.

N. B. The Trustees of the Library belonging to the late Exeter Academy met on the 21st instant to consider of the application referred to in the above Report.

Present, the Rev. MIC. TOWGOOD,
Rev. JOHN HOGG,
Rev. ABRAHAM TOZER,
Rev. J. P. BARTLETT,
Rev. JAMES MANNING.

Who unanimously agreed to grant the use of their Library to the New Academical Institution; at the same time presenting their compliments to the Gentlemen of the Committee, and assuring them that they wish them every degree of success in the present undertaking, that they are happy to have it in their power to oblige them, and that they shall always hold themselves under continued obligations to do all they can to forward so laudable a Design.

The following is a copy of a Vote of thanks passed at the half-yearly Assembly of Protestant Dissenting Ministers, held at Exeter on the 10th of May last, transmitted by the Moderator of that Assembly to Thomas Rogers. Esq.

Resolved,

THAT the thanks of this Assembly be returned to the Gentlemen of the Committee of the New Academical Institution for their attention to the state of
the

the Diſſenting Intereſt, and their vigorous exertions to ſupport it. That the Moderator be deſired to communicate the thanks of the Aſſembly to the Committee, and at the ſame time expreſs our approbation of the general plan of the New Inſtitution, and our wiſhes for its ſucceſs.

(Signed)

JAMES MANNING, Moderator.

REPORT, &c.

КIОРЪ,

REPORT, &c.

London, *January* 17, 1787.

AT a numerous and respectable Meeting of the Governors and Subscribers to the New ACADEMICAL INSTITUTION among Protestant Dissenters, for the education of their Ministers and Youth, THOMAS ROGERS, Esq. was called to the Chair; and the following Report from the Committee was read: viz.

GENTLEMEN,

AGREEABLY to the third Resolution of the 10th of March, 1786, that a General Annual Meeting be held on the third Wednesday of January in each year, to elect Officers, receive Reports, and transact other business respecting the New Academical Institution, your Committee have now called you together.

Sensible of the great importance and utility of the design, which you have authorized them to carry into execution, your Committee have been anxious to discharge their trust with fidelity and zeal, and have been unremitting in their endeavours to accelerate the completion of an Institution, which promises the most beneficial effects with regard to the rising generation, and the general interests of truth, piety, virtue, and religious liberty.

The necessity of hiring suitable apartments for the purpose of giving Lectures to such Divinity Students as the Committee might think proper to encourage, until the Institution be fixed in a house capable of admitting Lay-students as well as others, has been superseded by the kindness

kindness of the Trustees of Dr. Daniel Williams's Library, who have unanimously consented to grant us the use of a room in that library during the present year.

Accordingly the Academical business commenced, in the beginning of October, with five Divinity Students, besides one who is upon his own foundation. To those encouraged by your exhibitions, another, well recommended, hath this month been added. The Tutors have regularly carried on a course of Lectures to the Students six days in the week. They are also instructed, one day in the week, in the principles and practice of elocution; a subject of much consequence to those, who are intended to be public speakers.

Justice to the young men under your patronage, requires our informing you, that their abilities and application, as well as their religious and moral conduct, give us reason to expect, that by their future usefulness they will do honour to your generous encouragement and support.

With regard to the grand object of providing an Academical House, or College, your Committee have bestowed upon it the most assiduous attention. They have examined every place in the vicinity of the Metropolis which might, in their opinion, be likely to answer your views. They entered into several negociations for the purchase of houses or for procuring a proper spot of ground, and they obtained from Mr. Blackburn, an able Surveyor and Architect, and a zealous friend to the present undertaking, the plan of a commodious building.

After a variety of endeavours, and much enquiry and deliberation, they have been induced to give a decided preference to the house and land in the parish of Hackney, which they have purchased for the use of the Institution, and which they have reason to believe, will be found adequate to your wishes.

The house is a large and noble building, and in the most substantial repair. The land belonging to it, and in which it stands, is computed to consist of about eighteen acres, enclosed within a brick wall. The walks, garden ground, offices, and other conveniences, correspond in every respect to the house itself. The situation is in a
healthful

healthful and gravelly soil, well watered, and affording agreeable and extensive prospects. The principal apartments of the house are admirably accommodated for a library, lecture rooms, and the public meetings of the friends of the Institution. It is also, in its present state, capable of admitting a number of pupils: but as other buildings will be requisite for accommodating such a number of Students as there is reason to expect will be offered, it is necessary to erect an additional wing, which it is proposed to execute as speedily as possible. The purchase of this valuable freehold, with the fixtures, timber, and other articles upon it, has been five thousand six hundred pounds; a sum which enters deeply into the funds of the Society. But large as this sum is, when it is considered, that an entire new building, with the land necessary for it, properly enclosed and laid out for the domestic and other uses of the Institution, would have been much more expensive; that there was an extreme difficulty in procuring a suitable spot of ground; and that it would have required two or three years before the edifice could have been fitted for use:—When it is farther considered that this purchase is in the most desirable situation which could have been selected; that it has a respectable and collegiate appearance; that it is adapted to the convenient attendance of tutors, governors, and visitors; that it is well calculated for the preservation of discipline; that it is near to such different places of worship, as may be agreeable to the inclinations and choice of the Students, or of their Parents and Guardians; and that it has in it every capability of improvement, to whatever degree of extent and dignity the Institution may hereafter arrive; your Committee have a full confidence that their conduct will receive your unanimous approbation; and that your zeal and that of the other friends to this great object will be exerted to give it the most effectual and liberal support.

Your Committee, having been happy in attaining so important a point, have the satisfaction of informing you, that they have succeeded in another matter, of no little consequence. They have engaged for Assistant resident Tutor, the Rev. John Kiddle, of Tiverton, Devonshire; an elderly gentleman of acknowledged abilities and excellent character, and of an amiable temper, who has long been employed in the bufinefs of education, and who is not only well acquainted with the Greek and Latin languages, but alfo with the modern tongues. This gentleman, by being always upon the fpot, befides attending to the order of the family, will be able to give effectual aid to your other Claffical Tutor, in bringing the Younger Students forward in that fpecies of literature; an object which your Committee have very much at heart. Mrs. Kiddle, the wife of Mr. Kiddle, who is excellently fitted for the purpofe by her prudence and experience, as well as by her active and cheerful difpofition, is chofen houfe-keeper, under the direction of the Committee, who take upon themfelves the care of the commons. Your Committee have the farther hope of engaging, as foon as proper accommodations can be provided, Dr. Rees to be Superintending Refident Tutor.

By thefe arrangements, and others to be farther adopted (in the future appointment of a Mathematical and Philofophical Tutor), in procuring all the neceffary means of important and ufeful inftruction, and in forming a proper fyftem of internal regulation and difcipline, your Committee hope to eftablifh, upon the foundation already laid, fuch an Inftitution, as will not only furnifh a requifite fupply of Minifters, but qualify young Gentlemen for filling the various ftations and offices of civil life with dignity and ufefulnefs. This, they apprehend, to be an object of fingular importance; and no meafure that can contribute to the attainment of it, fhall be difregarded.

They have the additional pleafure of acquainting you, that Mrs. Harris, of Honiton, Devonfhire, widow of the late Rev. and learned Dr. William Harris, the author of feveral hiftorical works, hath made a prefent to the New Academical Inftitution of her hufband's Library, containing many curious publications. This generous donation, and the ufe of the Exeter Library already obtained, your Committee regard as pleafing aufpices that future inftances will occur of fimilar generofity;—a large and well furnifhed library being highly conducive to the honour and utility of the Inftitution.

Agreeably

Agreeably to former Refolutions of the general body of the Subfcribers, your Committee have proceeded in eftablifhing a permanent fund, and prepared a proper deed of truft for this purpofe. And they now report to you that the fum of £. 2,332, 5s. being the third part of the amount of the benefactions received in the laft year, hath been paffed or placed to the account of the faid fund in purfuance of the 3d Refolution of the 21ft of July laft. They beg leave to add, that the prefent amount of benefactions, fubfcriptions, and dividends on ftock, the greateft part of which has been received, is £. 8,547, 9s.

Thus far your Committee have been enabled to proceed; and they are happy in having fo agreeable a profpect before them. They are fenfible that much yet remains to be done; that many regulations are to be eftablifhed, and various meafures to be purfued, previoufly to the opening of the College at Michaelmas next. To thefe things they will zealoufly and diligently apply; and, when prepared, will take the liberty of convening you again, and laying before you an account of their proceedings.

While your Committee exprefs their moft grateful fenfe of the generous fupport with which the defign hath already been favoured, they beg leave to add, that farther aid is requifite to carry it on to perfection; and this aid they have the full confidence of receiving from the nature, importance, and extent of the Inftitution, and the munificent fpirit of its friends and patrons. Several refpectable perfons have added their names, fince the laft lift of benefactors and fubfcribers was printed:—And there can be no doubt but that others will come forward on this great occafion;—the greateft occafion, which hath ever called forth the attention and the ardour of the liberal-minded among the Proteftant Diffenters; and one of the greateft occafions that has ever been prefented to the friends, in general, of truth and piety, of an enlarged and virtuous education, and of civil and religious liberty.

The

The Report having been read, the following Resolutions were moved and UNANIMOUSLY agreed to, viz.

I. THAT the Thanks of this Meeting be given to the Committee for the measures they have taken, as now reported; and particularly for the purchase, so judiciously made, at Hackney, for the use of the Institution, which we highly approve of for the situation of our intended College, and which appears in other respects so well to correspond with the magnitude and importance of the objects which we have in view.

II. THAT the Committee be instructed to make such immediate addition to the house lately purchased at Hackney as they shall judge to be necessary for the proper opening of the College in September next, and to take such other measures as shall appear to them to be requisite for carrying their whole plan into execution.

III. THAT the Thanks of this Meeting be given to the Trustees of the Exeter Library for their granting the use of it to this Institution.

IV. THAT the Thanks of this Meeting be given to Mrs. Harris, widow of the late Rev. Dr. William Harris, for her very valuable present of his Library.

V. A doubt having arisen as to the meaning of the Resolution under which the General Committee was appointed in July last, Resolved THAT the present Committee be continued till the third Wednesday in January next.

VI. THAT the Thanks of this Meeting be given to the Chairman.

(Signed)
THOMAS ROGERS, Chairman.

N. B. Subscriptions for this Institution will be received by the Chairman, or any other Gentleman of the Committee.

LONDON, *March* 21, 1787.

SIR,

THE Committee for establishing the New ACADEMICAL INSTITUTION have now the pleasure of transmitting to you a farther Report of their proceedings, together with the Resolutions of the General Meeting of Subscribers held on the 17th of January. The information contained in this Report would have been communicated sooner, if the Committee had not been desirous of giving you, at the same time, an account of the measures that have been adopted in pursuance of these Resolutions. By the Report you will find, that the house lately purchased is excellently adapted in a variety of respects to the purposes of the Institution. Besides the rooms, which will be appropriated to the library, lectures, and public exercises, as well as to domestic use, it contains several other very commodious apartments, which will be allotted for the reception of Students. These are spacious and airy; and being fit for immediate residence, the Committee will have it in their power to accommodate, at the opening of the session in September next, a considerable number of Young Gentlemen intended for civil and commercial life, besides those designed for the Ministry; of which they take this early opportunity to inform their friends. Their terms of admission will soon be announced to the public.

But as there is reason to expect a much greater number of Students than the house in its present state will admit, the Committee, in consequence of the Resolutions of the last General Meeting, have given orders for the addition of a new wing, consisting of several ranges of lodging-rooms and studies, which will be executed with all convenient dispatch. The plan is already formed by Mr. Blackburn, and a Sub-committee is appointed for superintending the execution of it, under his direction, and agreeably to an estimate which he has delivered. We have the pleasure to add, that the proposed building has been much approved not only by the General Committee, but by many other friends of the Institution,

Inſtitution, to whom the deſign has been communicated. The wing now undertaken is, indeed, only part of a plan, which we hope to ſee executed, in its utmoſt extent, at ſome future period, by the generous patronage of the public. We have ordered the plan and elevation of the building to be engraved, copies of which will be ſent to the Subſcribers as ſoon as they are finiſhed, that the moſt diſtant friends of the Inſtitution may be able to form a judgment of our whole deſign, and be induced to unite with us in their wiſhes and exertions for its completion.

With that general concurrence which we may reaſonably expect, we have no doubt of accompliſhing the great object in view; and of eſtabliſhing an Inſtitution, the utility of which will be extenſive and permanent.

Whilſt the Committee have been anxious to provide ſuitable accommodations for the Young Gentlemen, who may offer, they have been no leſs aſſiduous in their endeavours to lay the foundation of ſuch government and diſcipline as may be effectual for preſerving their virtue and reputation. They have the pleaſure of informing you, that with this view, they have prevailed on Dr. Rees to accept the office of Reſident Tutor, and to take the direction and government of the Inſtitution. A houſe contiguous to the main building is now preparing for his accommodation, and will be ready at the opening of the ſeſſion.

The Committee are alſo digeſting a ſyſtem of internal regulations, derived as far as they are able to collect them from the wiſdom and experience of thoſe, who have been connected with ſimilar Inſtitutions.

They are determined moreover, to provide, at all times, ſuitable means of inſtruction in the various branches of Literature and Science.

Upon the whole they indulge the hope, that the ſituation of the New Inſtitution, and the advantages that accompany it with regard to health, morals, and mental improvement, will render it adequate in importance and uſe to the juſt expectations of its liberal founders, and recommend it to the patronage of the friends of truth and virtue, of their country, and of mankind.

The

The Committee beg leave to add, that the completion of the plan which they have adopted will require farther assistance; nor have they any fear that their design will fail for want of encouragement and support. They are solicitous to avoid both the extremes of parsimony and profusion; and to approve themselves to the friends of the Institution by such exertions at its first establishment as may be likely to contribute to its credit and success.

It is the highest ambition of the Committee to be faithful to their trust; and to apply the donations and subscriptions, committed to their disposal, in such a manner to the support of this Institution, as shall appear to their deliberate judgment the most effectual for the advancement and prosperity of the cause of Truth and Liberty, and for the reputation and advantage of the rising generation. These are the great objects to which their own views, in concurrence with those of the other friends of the Institution, are directed; and to the attainment of these objects they devote a very considerable portion of their time and labour. Happy, therefore, in the consciousness of their own integrity and zeal, and encouraged by the appprobation of those who are best acquainted with the measures they are pursuing, they confide in your continued assistance.

We are, Sir, with great respect,

Your most humble Servants,

Signed, by order of the Committee,

THOMAS ROGERS, Chairman.

NEW ACADEMICAL INSTITUTION.

THE Committee for establishing the NEW ACADEMICAL INSTITUTION among Protestant Dissenters, for the education of Ministers and Youth, have now the pleasure to inform the public, that the spacious and eligible house, which they have purchased in the parish of Hackney, will be opened for the reception of Students, on the 29th day of September next. The situation of this house is recommended by a variety of local conveniences and advantages; and the Committee will assiduously avail themselves of every circumstance that may be conducive to the health, moral conduct, and literary improvement of the young Gentlemen, who shall be entrusted to their care. They beg leave to add, that it is a fundamental principle of this Institution, that it will be open to persons of all Denominations, who will be encouraged in forming their religious sentiments without restriction or imposition.

The course of education will be comprehensive and liberal, and adapted to youth in general, whether they are intended for civil or commercial life, or for any of the learned professions. This course will include the Latin, Greek, and Hebrew Languages, Greek and Roman Antiquities, Ancient and Modern Geography, Universal Grammar, Rhetoric and Composition, Chronology,

nology, History, Civil and Ecclesiastical, the Principles of Law and Government, the several Branches of Mathematics, Astronomy, Natural and Experimental Philosophy and Chemistry, Logic, Metaphysics and Ethics, the Evidences of Religion, Natural and Revealed, Theology, Jewish Antiquities, and Critical Lectures on the Scriptures.

The Gentlemen who have engaged to conduct this plan of education, are, the

    Rev. RICHARD PRICE, D. D. F. R. S.
    Rev. ANDREW KIPPIS, D. D. F. R. S. and S. A.
    Rev. ABRAHAM REES, D. D. F. R. S.
    Rev. HUGH WORTHINGTON.
    Rev. GEORGE CADOGAN MORGAN.
    Rev. JOHN KIDDLE.

The Students will be instructed in the practice of Elocution, by a person appointed for that purpose.

The usual course for young Gentlemen not intended for the ministry, will be compleated in three years; and with respect to those who shall continue longer in college, a proper plan of education will be pursued.

The commons will be provided by the Committee; and the Students will be under the more immediate direction and government of Dr. Rees, who will reside in a house contiguous to the main building, and of Mr. Kiddle, who will live in the college with the students.

The terms for each session, commencing on the third Monday in September, and closing on the first day of July, are sixty guineas, which will include apartments, board, and education. Students on the foundation

will

will be provided for in thefe refpects without expence: And the Committee will encourage young perfons intended for the miniftry, whofe friends are willing to defray the charges of their board and education, by a confiderable abatement in the above terms.

It is fcarcely neceffary to obferve, that the fituation of this Inftitution affords opportunity of obtaining the beft means of inftruction in French and other Modern Languages, Drawing, &c. at a feparate expence.

No Divinity-ftudents will be admitted under the age of fixteen years; nor any Lay-ftudents under the age of fifteen years, nor above the age of eighteen years: and it is expected, that all ftudents be well recommended both as to conduct and qualifications.

Applications for the admiffion of ftudents may be made to

Thomas Rogers, Efq; Cornhill,
Matthew Towgood, Efq; Clement's-lane,
Michael Dodfon, Efq; Bofwell-court, Carey-ftreet,
} Treafurers.

Dr. Price, Hackney,
Dr. Kippis, Crown-ftreet, Weftminfter,
Dr. Rees, Old Jewry,
Rev. H. Worthington, Iflington.

LONDON, *April* 24, 1787.

N. B. Subfcriptions for this Inftitution will be received by the Treafurers, or any other Gentleman of the Committee.

nology, History, Civil and Ecclesiastical, the Principles of Law and Government, the several Branches of Mathematics, Astronomy, Natural and Experimental Philosophy and Chemistry, Logic, Metaphysics and Ethics, the Evidences of Religion, Natural and Revealed, Theology, Jewish Antiquities, and Critical Lectures on the Scriptures.

The Gentlemen who have engaged to conduct this plan of education, are, the
    Rev. RICHARD PRICE, D. D. F. R. S.
    Rev. ANDREW KIPPIS, D. D. F. R. S. and S. A.
    Rev. ABRAHAM REES, D. D. F. R. S.
    Rev. HUGH WORTHINGTON.
    Rev. GEORGE CADOGAN MORGAN.
    Rev. JOHN KIDDLE.

The Students will be instructed in the practice of Elocution, by a person appointed for that purpose.

The usual course for young Gentlemen not intended for the ministry, will be compleated in three years; and with respect to those who shall continue longer in college, a proper plan of education will be pursued.

The commons will be provided by the Committee; and the Students will be under the more immediate direction and government of Dr. Rees, who will reside in a house contiguous to the main building, and of Mr. Kiddle, who will live in the college with the students.

The terms for each session, commencing on the third Monday in September, and closing on the first day of July, are sixty guineas, which will include apartments, board, and education. Students on the foundation
                                        will

will be provided for in thefe refpects without expence: And the Committee will encourage young perfons intended for the miniftry, whofe friends are willing to defray the charges of their board and education, by a confiderable abatement in the above terms.

It is fcarcely neceffary to obferve, that the fituation of this Inftitution affords opportunity of obtaining the beft means of inftruction in French and other Modern Languages, Drawing, &c. at a feparate expence.

No Divinity-ftudents will be admitted under the age of fixteen years; nor any Lay-ftudents under the age of fifteen years, nor above the age of eighteen years: and it is expected, that all ftudents be well recommended both as to conduct and qualifications.

Applications for the admiffion of ftudents may be made to
Thomas Rogers, Efq; Cornhill,
Matthew Towgood, Efq; Clement's-lane, } Treafurers.
Michael Dodfon, Efq; Bofwell-court, Carey-ftreet,
Dr. Price, Hackney,
Dr. Kippis, Crown-ftreet, Weftminfter,
Dr. Rees, Old Jewry,
Rev. H. Worthington, Iflington.
LONDON, *April* 24, 1787.

N. B. Subfcriptions for this Inftitution will be received by the Treafurers, or any other Gentleman of the Committee.

www.ingramcontent.com/pod-product-compliance
Lightning Source LLC
Chambersburg PA
CBHW020302090426
42735CB00009B/1190